THE HUMAN BODY

Carron Brown

Illustrated by Rachael Saunders

Kane Miller
A DIVISION OF EDC PUBLISHING

A human body has many
parts that work together to
help a person live and grow.

If you look closely at people eating,
moving, breathing, talking and playing,
you will see their bodies working.

Shine a flashlight behind the page,
or hold it up to the light to see inside
the human body. Discover a hidden
world of great surprises.

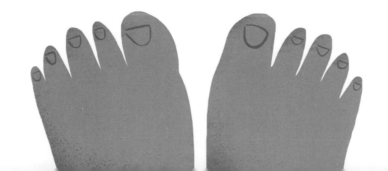

A new person is
waiting to be born.

Can you see her?

Aaah!

Here she is!

The baby is growing
in her mother's belly.
She stays there for
nine months until she
is ready to be born.

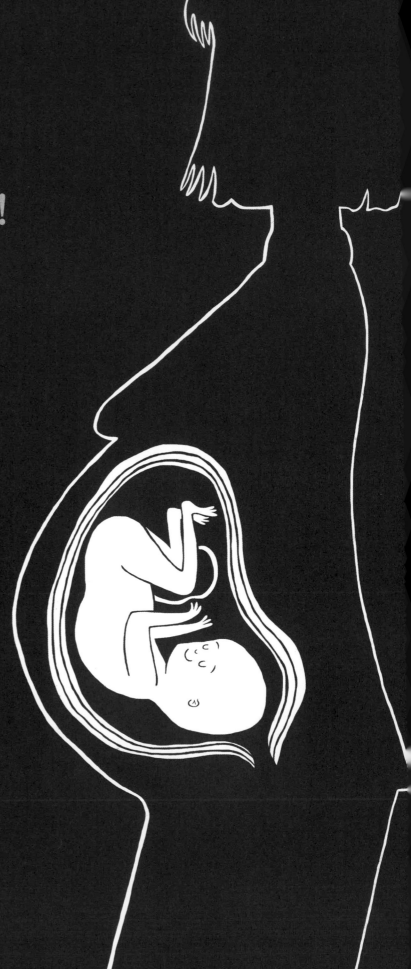

A child slowly grows bigger, until he or she becomes an adult.

Do you know what is growing inside these children's bodies, underneath their skin?

Stretch!

Bones! More than 200 of them are joined together in a frame called a skeleton, which helps the body stay strong as it gets bigger.

This girl has run very fast to catch up with the ball.

What makes her body move?

The muscles that are joined to her skeleton pull on her bones to make her body move.

Goal!

Skin covers and protects the body.

On our fingertips, the skin forms special patterns. Can you see them on this girl's hand?

Swirls and whorls cover the fingertips. These skin patterns are called fingerprints. Every person's fingerprints are different.

Wiggle!

Air comes into the body through the nose and the mouth.

Where does it go next?

The air is sucked into the lungs. The oxygen in the air keeps the body alive.

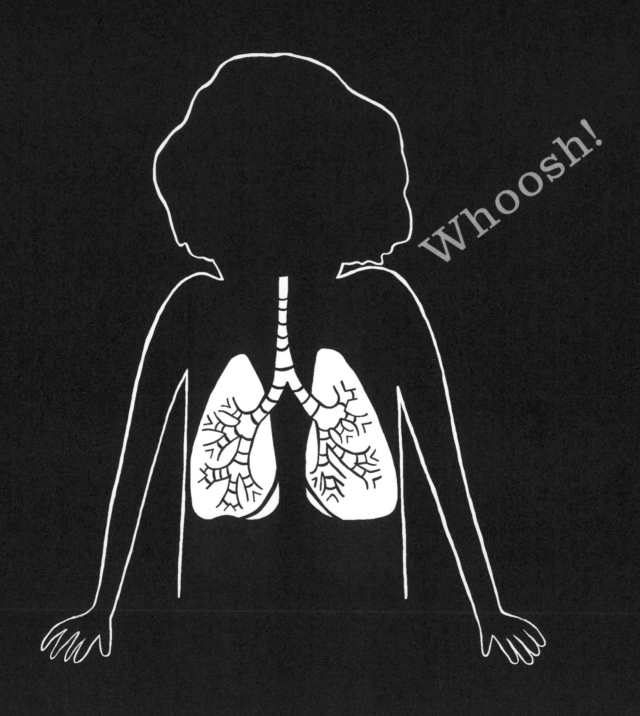

Air travels all through the body. It is carried by the blood.

How does the blood move through the body?

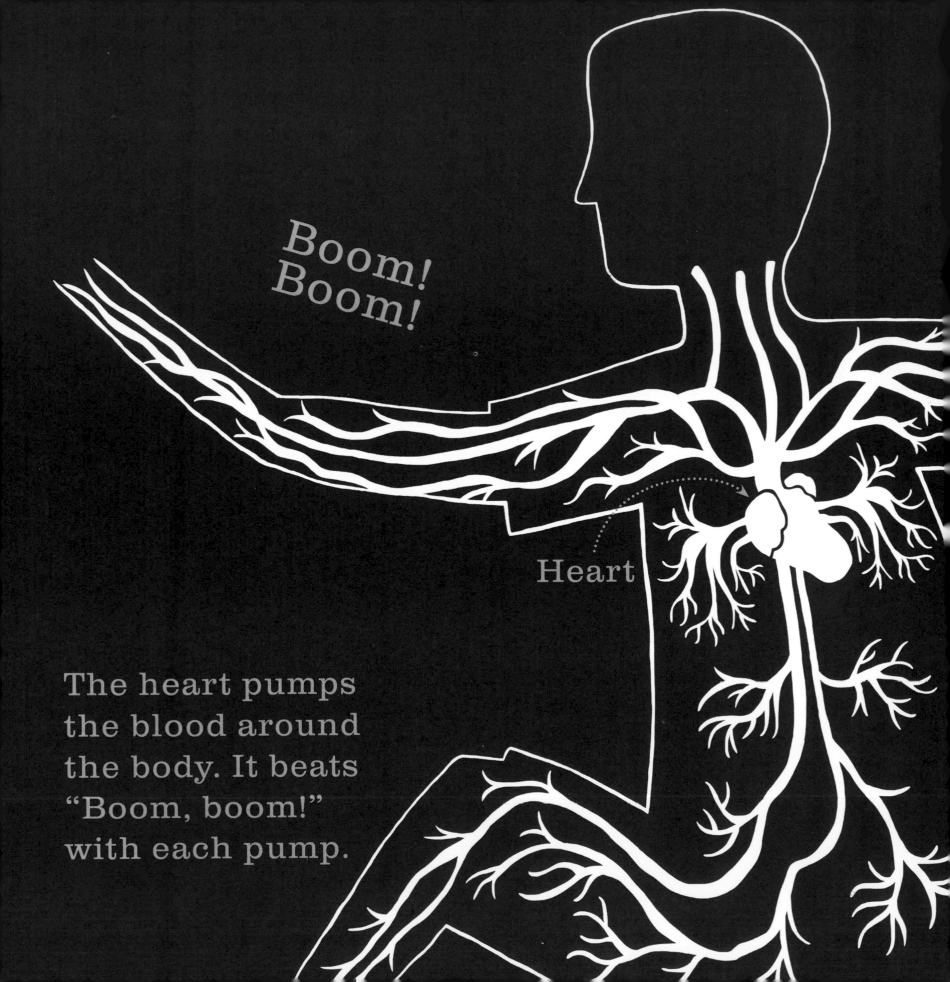

Purr! This cat's fur feels soft. The boy knows this because sensors in his skin send messages to his brain about what he is touching.

Where is his brain?

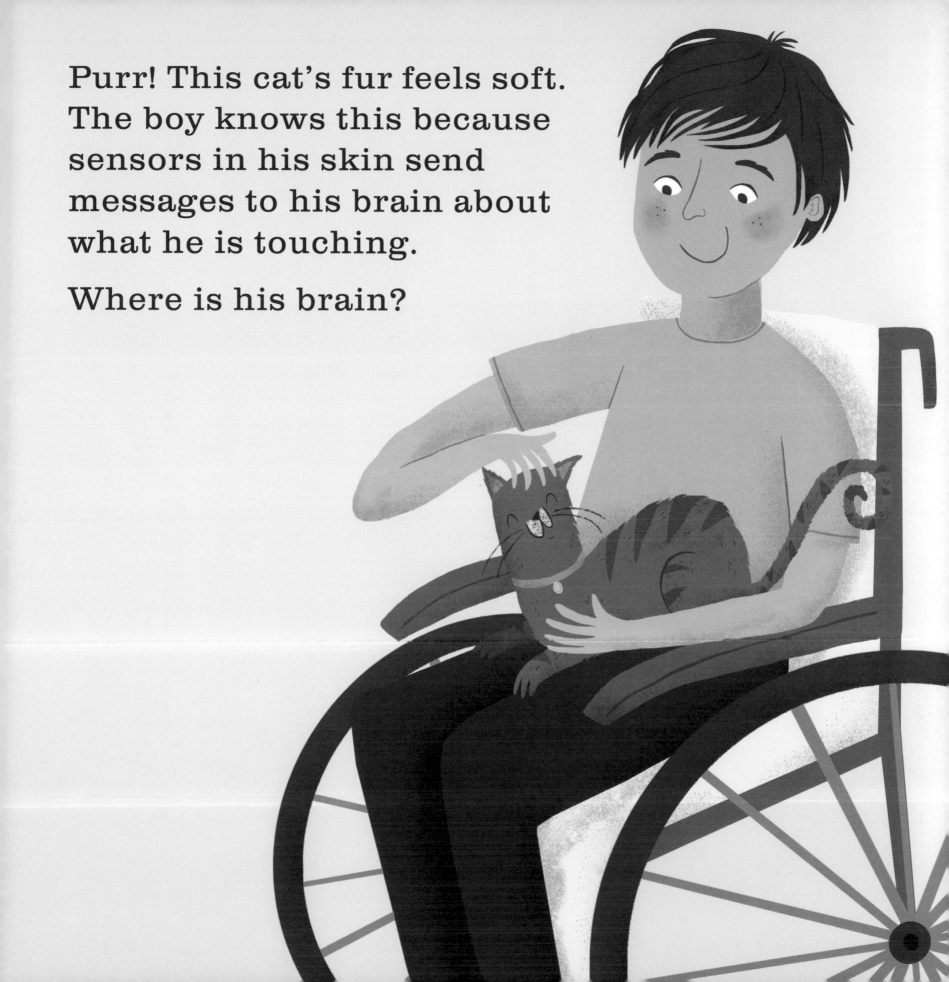

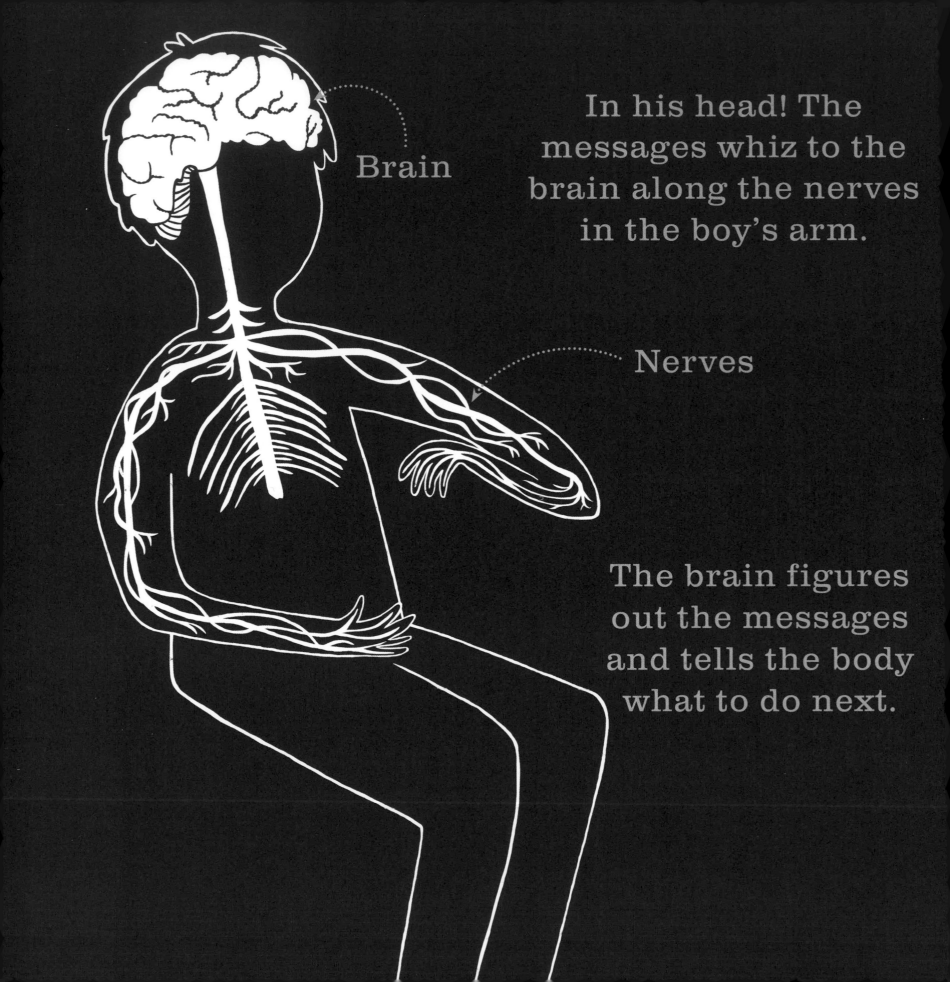

Brain

In his head! The messages whiz to the brain along the nerves in the boy's arm.

Nerves

The brain figures out the messages and tells the body what to do next.

The body has five senses that tell it about the world. These are sight, hearing, touch, smell and taste.

Which senses is this boy using?

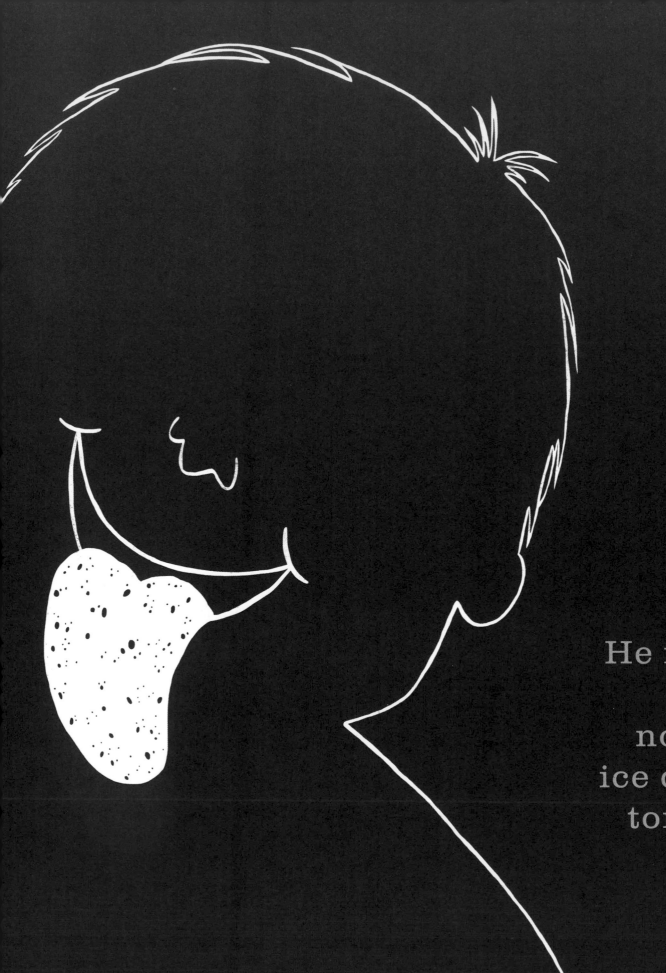

Yum!

He is using smell and taste. His nose smells the ice cream and his tongue tastes it.

The busy human body needs energy to stay active. We get this energy from food.

What happens to food after it's been swallowed?

The food travels down
a tube to the stomach.
Then it squeezes through
a longer, winding tube,
called the intestines.

Stomach

Intestines

The body uses the
food for energy. Any
food that can't be used
leaves the body as poop.

Eating lots of healthy foods helps the body to stay well.

What's inside this basket?

Vegetables, fruit, fish, cheese and bread. These foods each have different nutrients that keep the body healthy.

Munch! Crunch!

Drinking plenty of water helps to keep the body healthy. But the body must get rid of the water it doesn't need.

How does this happen?

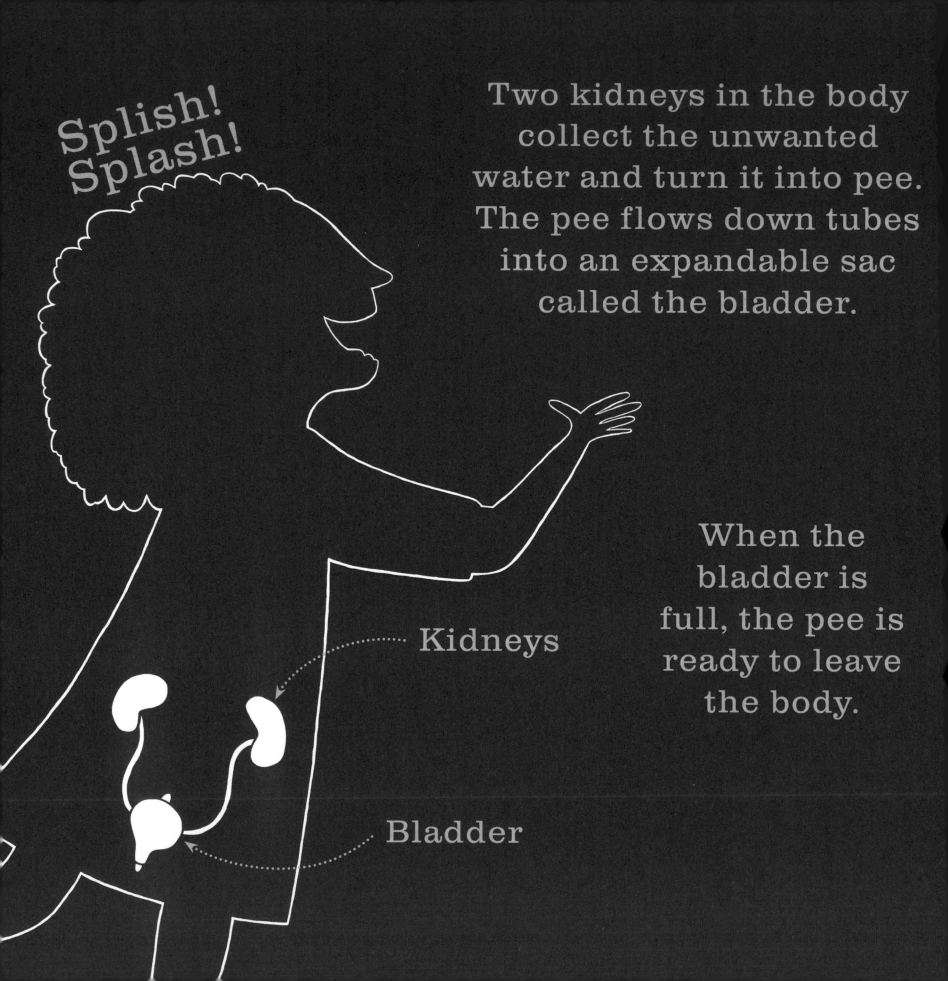

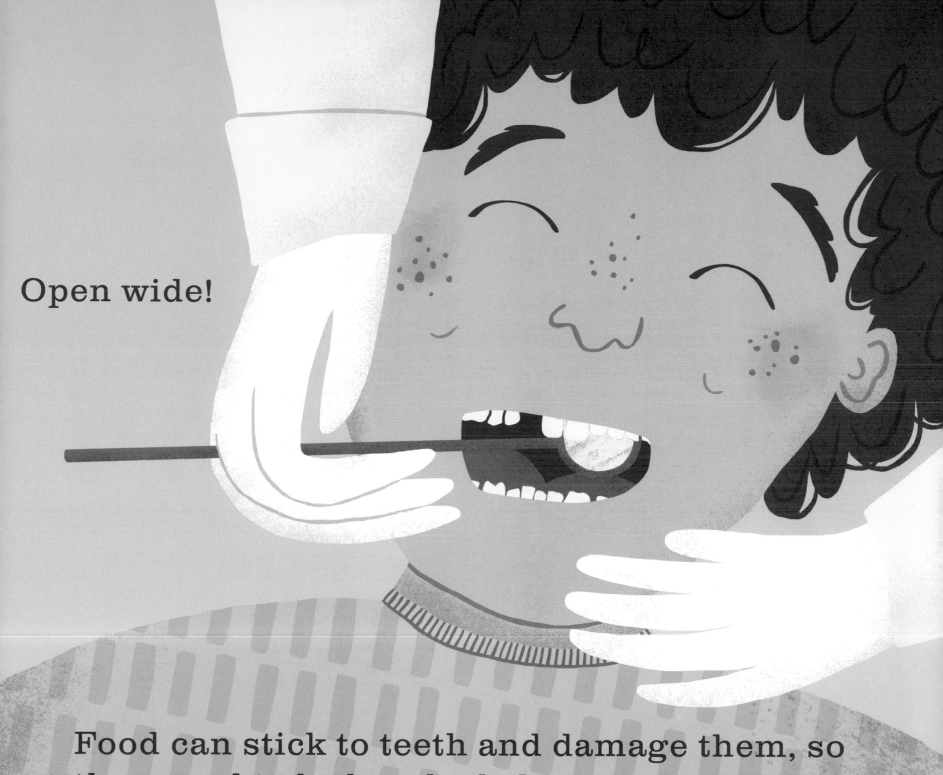

Open wide!

Food can stick to teeth and damage them, so they need to be brushed clean. A dentist is checking this boy's teeth.

Do you know what is going to fill in the gap?

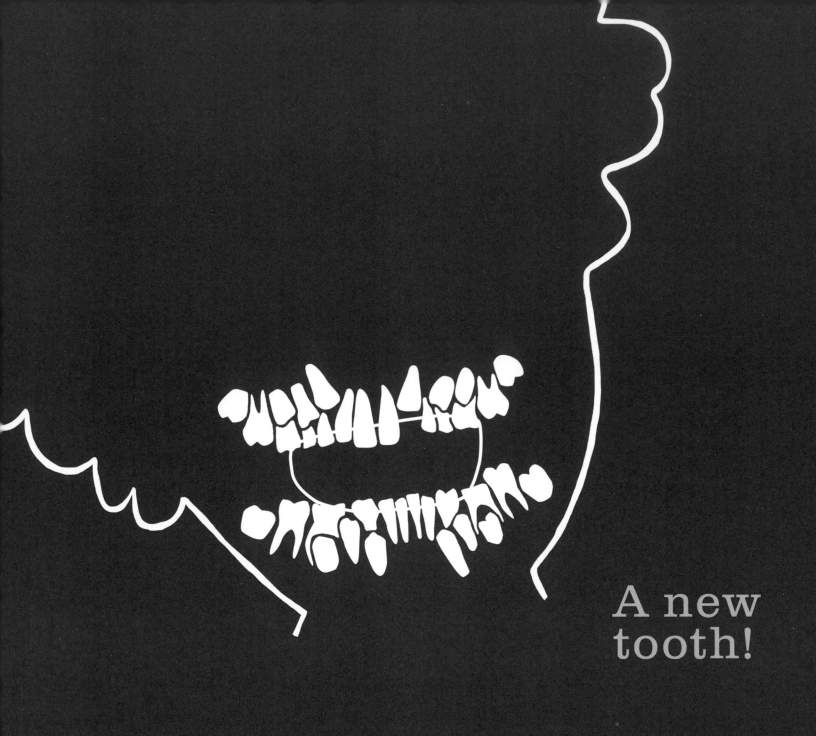

A new
tooth!

First teeth are called baby teeth. As the
body grows, each baby tooth is pushed out
by a larger, adult tooth. There are 20 baby
teeth and 32 adult teeth.

If harmful germs get inside the body they can make us ill. The body can fight off most germs by itself, but sometimes a doctor's help is needed.

This doctor is holding a thermometer. What will it show?

The thermometer shows the body's temperature.

99.0 °F

A number higher than 99 tells the doctor that the body is fighting hard to get rid of the germs—and might need medicine.

This girl is at the hospital. She has fallen down and hurt her arm. The doctor used an X-ray machine to take a picture of her arm bones.

Can you see the X-ray?

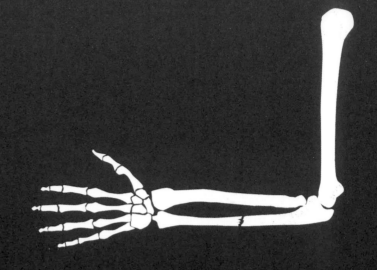

Ouch!

One bone is broken. The doctor will put a hard cast around the arm. This will keep it still until the broken bone has mended.

Bodies need rest. When we are sleeping, it might seem like not much is happening, but the body is still quite busy.

What is going on inside this boy's brain?

Dreams!

Dreams happen when the brain puts together all kinds of different thoughts.

The human body is so amazing that it can even make a new brother or sister for you!

There's more...

The body has lots of different jobs to do. Read more
about some of the parts of the body that are in this book.

Skeleton The skeleton is a frame of connected bones that
shapes a body. Joints, such as ankles, elbows and hips, are
where bones join together and allow the body to bend.

Muscles Flexible muscles help a person move. Most
muscles are attached to the skeleton and work in pairs
to move it. Muscles pull on bones to make them move.

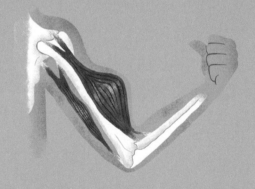

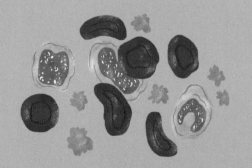

Blood Blood is a liquid made up of tiny cells. Red blood
cells carry oxygen, while white blood cells kill germs.

Lungs Air containing a gas called oxygen is breathed in
and fills the lungs, which inflate like balloons. Blood flowing
through the lungs collects the oxygen. As waste gases are
breathed out, the lungs deflate and get smaller.

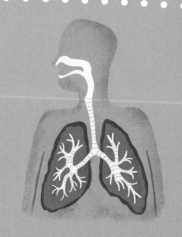

Heart The heart is a muscle that beats nonstop to pump blood throughout the body. Blood flows through tubes called arteries and veins.

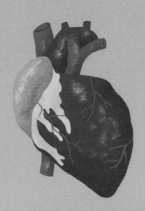

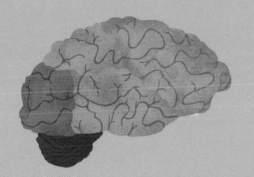

Brain The brain is where thoughts and feelings come from. It controls the muscles, as well as some actions such as breathing and heartbeat, which take place without us having to think about them.

Stomach The stomach is a stretchy, bag-like body part that food goes into after it is swallowed. Muscles in the stomach move to break down the food and turn it into mush.

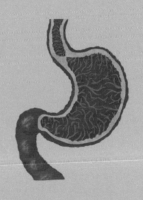

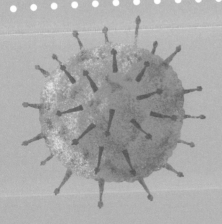

Germs Germs are tiny bacteria and viruses that can make us ill. Sometimes medicine is needed to help the body fight the germs.

First American Edition 2016
Kane Miller, A Division of EDC Publishing

Copyright © 2017 Quarto Publishing plc

Published by arrangement with Ivy Kids, an imprint of The Quarto Group.
All rights reserved. No part of this book may be reproduced, transmitted
or stored in an information retrieval system in any form or by any means,
graphic, electronic or mechanical, including photocopying, taping and
recording, without prior written permission from the publisher.

For information contact:
Kane Miller, A Division of EDC Publishing
PO Box 470663
Tulsa, OK 74147-0663
www.kanemiller.com
www.edcpub.com
www.usbornebooksandmore.com

Library of Congress Control Number: 2015954203

Printed in China

ISBN: 978-1-61067-465-2